Contents

Words written in bold, **like this,** are explained in the Glossary.

 Find out more about space at www.heinemannexplore.co.uk.

What is the Moon?

The Moon is a huge ball of rock and metal that **orbits** the Earth. It is Earth's **satellite**. A satellite is something that orbits a planet.

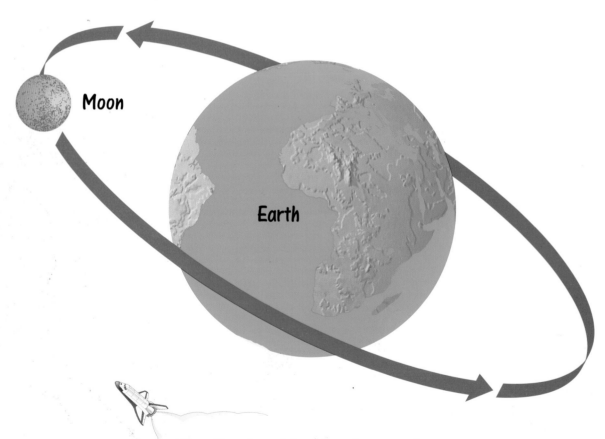

Moon

Earth

The Earth orbits the Sun and the Moon orbits the Earth.

Space Explorer

THE MOON

Patricia Whitehouse

Heinemann
LIBRARY

Young
Explorer

4165 7175 21

 www.heinemann.co.uk/library
Visit our website to find out more information about *Heinemann Library* books.

To order:
 Phone ++44 (0)1865 888066
 Send a fax to ++44 (0)1865 314091
 Visit the Heinemann Bookshop at **www.heinemann.co.uk/library** to browse our catalogue and order online.

First published in Great Britain by Heinemann Library, Halley Court, Jordan Hill, Oxford OX2 8EJ, part of Harcourt Education. Heinemann is a registered trademark of Harcourt Education Ltd.

Editorial: Jilly Attwood and Kate Bellamy
Design: Ron Kamen and Paul Davies
Picture Research: Ruth Blair and Sally Claxton
Production: Séverine Ribierre
Originated by Dot Gradations
Printed and bound in China by South China Printing Company

The paper used to print this book comes from sustainable resources.

ISBN 0 431 11341 6
(hardback)
08 07 06 05 04
10 9 8 7 6 5 4 3 2 1

ISBN 0 431 11351 3
(paperback)
09 08 07 06 05
10 9 8 7 6 5 4 3 2 1

British Library Cataloguing in Publication Data
Whitehouse, Patricia
The Moon – (Space Explorer)
523.3
A full catalogue record for this book is available from the British Library.

Acknowledgements
The Publishers are grateful to the following for permission to reproduce photographs: Corbis pp. **7, 15, 18, 20** (royalty free); Getty Images/Photodisc pp. **5, 9, 10, 26**; NASA pp. **8, 11, 12, 13, 14, 17, 19, 27**; Oxford Scientific Films pp. **28, 29** (David Thompson); Science Photo Library pp. **16** (NASA), **22** (David Nunuk), **24, 25** (Eckhard Slawick)

Cover photo reproduced with permission of Bruce Coleman/C.S. Neilson.

Our thanks to Stuart Clark for his assistance in the preparation of this book.

Every effort has been made to contact copyright holders of any material reproduced in this book. Any omissions will be rectified in subsequent printings if notice is given to the Publishers.

One side of the
Moon always faces the
Earth. The other side
always faces away.
People on Earth can
only see one side
of the Moon.

The Moon is 3476 kilometres across. This is about four times smaller than the Earth. About 50 Moons could fit inside the Earth.

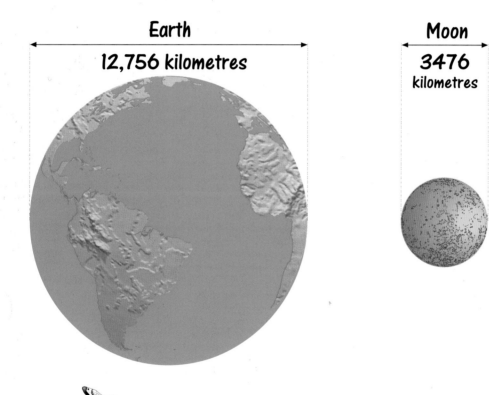

Earth
12,756 kilometres

Moon
3476 kilometres

Earth is about four times wider than the Moon.

Sometimes the Moon looks like it's about the size of your thumb. It looks small because it is 384,390 kilometres away.

A rocky surface

The Moon is made up of rocks, metals and dust. There is no water on the Moon. Scientists think ice might be buried beneath the Moon's **surface** near its north pole.

Astronauts brought back samples of different Moon rocks for scientists to study.

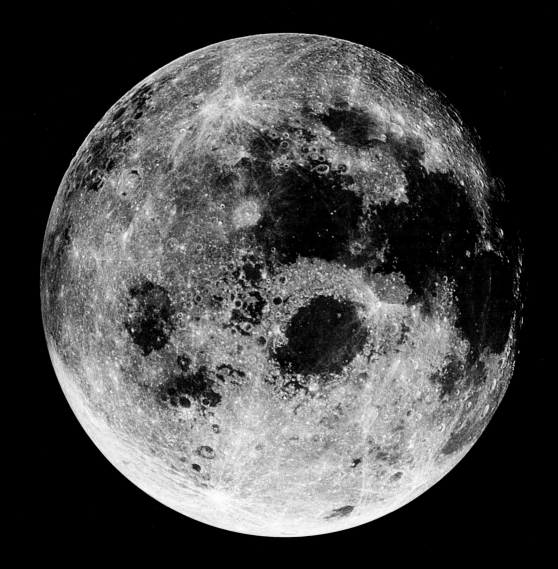

The dust on the Moon was made when **meteorites** crashed into it and broke rocks apart. The dark and light areas we can see show the Moon is made from different kinds of rocks.

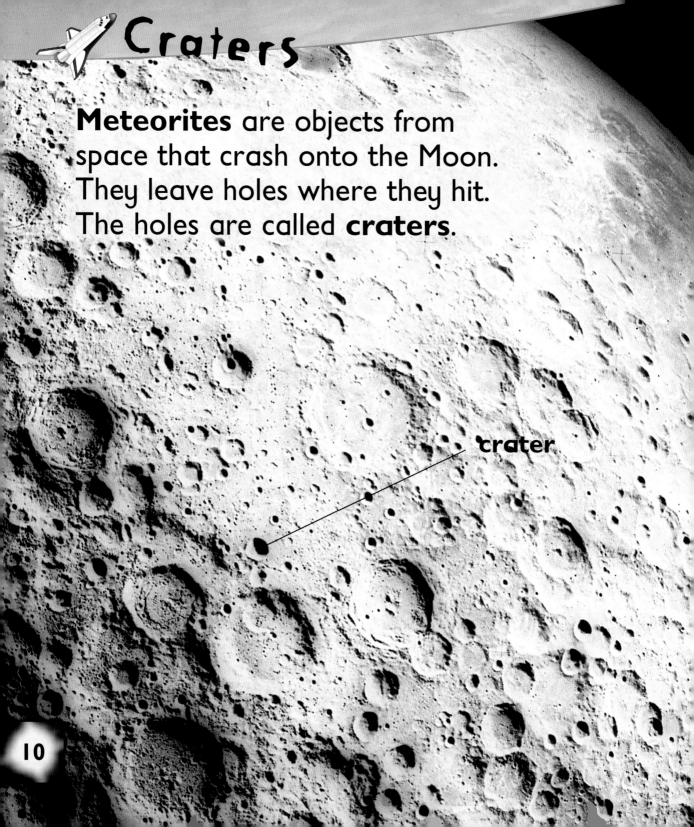

Craters

Meteorites are objects from space that crash onto the Moon. They leave holes where they hit. The holes are called **craters**.

crater

Aitken Basin

Craters can be a few millimetres or several hundred kilometres in size. The largest crater is called The Aitken Basin. It is 2250 kilometres across.

Long ago, people thought the dark parts of the Moon were seas of water. Now we know they were once **lava** flows. The dark patches are still called seas.

Sea of Serenity

Sea of Showers

Sea of Tranquility

Ocean of Storms

Sea of Fertility

Like the Earth, the Moon has valleys and mountains. The tallest Moon mountains are the Apennines which are about 6000 metres high.

The large mountain behind the astronaut is called Hadley Rille. The mountain to the left of it is Hadley Delta.

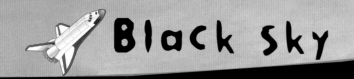

The Earth is covered by a layer of **gas** called the **atmosphere**. The Sun shining through this makes the sky look blue. The Moon does not have an atmosphere so the sky always looks black.

This astronaut footprint has not changed in over 35 years.

There is no weather on the Moon. This means that wind and rain do not change **craters** and other Moon features. They can stay the same for millions of years.

Hot and cold

The Moon is either very hot or very cold. The Sun's heat causes the Moon to reach 130°C. That's the temperature of a warm oven on Earth.

This is what the Sun looks like from the Moon.

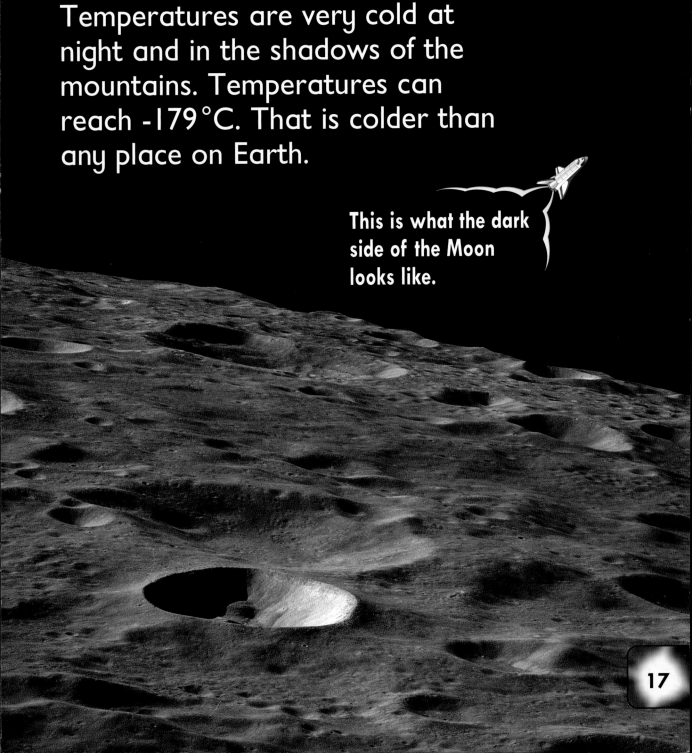

Temperatures are very cold at night and in the shadows of the mountains. Temperatures can reach -179°C. That is colder than any place on Earth.

This is what the dark side of the Moon looks like.

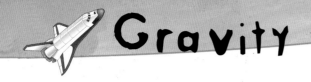

Gravity

Gravity is the force that pulls everything toward the centre of the Earth. It's why people and animals on Earth don't float away from the Earth's **surface**.

It takes a lot of energy to jump this high on Earth.

The Earth's gravity is about six times stronger than the Moon's gravity. On the Moon, you could jump six times higher than you can on Earth.

Even with heavy spacesuits, astronauts move around easily in the Moon's low gravity.

Moonlight

The Moon is the brightest object in our sky at night. But the Moon does not make its own light.

The Moon is lit up by the Sun.

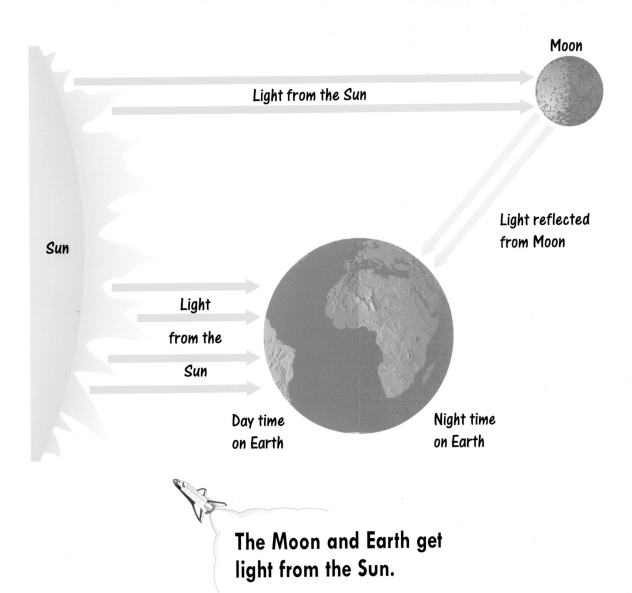

Moon

Light from the Sun

Light reflected from Moon

Sun

Light from the Sun

Day time on Earth

Night time on Earth

The Moon and Earth get light from the Sun.

Moonlight is really sunlight! The light from the Sun travels to the Moon. The sunlight bounces off the Moon's **surface**, and travels to the Earth.

Changing Shape

The Moon seems to change shape.
It goes from a whole moon to a thin
crescent, then back again. It takes 29 days
to do this and is called a lunar month.

When the Moon looks thin it is because we
can only see a bit of the side that is lit up.

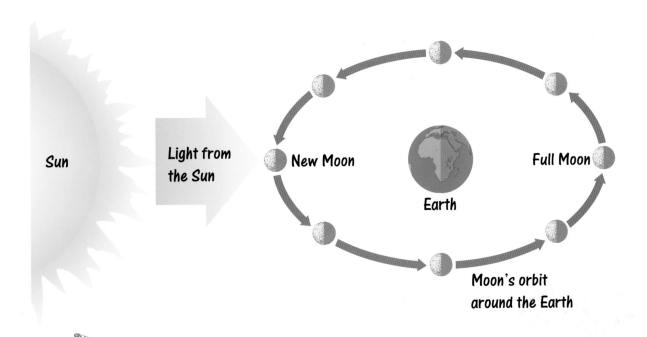

Sun

Light from the Sun

New Moon

Full Moon

Earth

Moon's orbit around the Earth

The Moon moves round the Earth and each night we see a different amount of the side that has sunlight on it.

The Moon's **orbit** around the Earth changes how much of the Moon we see. The shape of the Moon in our sky depends on how much sunlight is bounced towards the Earth.

Phases of the Moon

The changing shapes of the Moon are called **phases**. The **full moon** phase is a circle shape. Then the Moon gets smaller.

full moon

new moon

When the Moon is between the Sun and the Earth, we cannot see any **reflected** sunlight. The Moon cannot be seen. This is the **new moon** phase.

new
moon

Day and night

The Moon is not just up at night.
It is often up during the day.
We can sometimes see it
in the morning or in
the late afternoon.

The Moon coming up
is called moonrise.
The Moon going
down is called
moonset. Sometimes
the Moon looks
larger and orange
at moonrise.

**The space shuttle
Endeavour gets
ready to launch as
the Moon rises.**

Tides

The Moon's **gravity** pulls on the Earth's oceans. This causes the water level on shore to change. These changes of water levels are called tides.

At low tide, the Moon pulls the water away from the shore, so more of the shore shows. At high tide, the water moves back onto the shore.

Amazing Moon facts

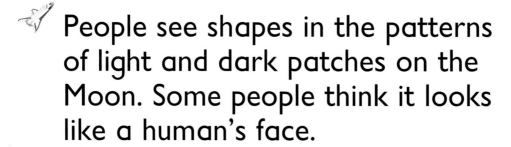 People see shapes in the patterns of light and dark patches on the Moon. Some people think it looks like a human's face.

Twelve astronauts have landed on the Moon.

Astrononauts brought 382 kilograms of Moon rocks back to Earth.

The Moon's **craters** have names. Many of the craters are named after famous scientists.

 Find out more about space at www.heinemannexplore.co.uk.

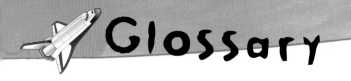 Glossary

atmosphere thick layer of gas around a planet

crater a hole caused by a meteorite hitting the surface of a planet, moon, or other object

full moon phase of the Moon that is a circle shape

gas air-like material that is not solid or liquid

gravity a force that pulls objects together

lava melted rock

meteorite an object from space, made of stone or metal, that crashes onto a planet or moon

new moon phase of the Moon where the Moon cannot be seen

orbit the path one object takes around another

phase one part of a cycle

reflect bounce off

satellite an object that orbits a planet or a moon

surface the top or outside of an object

More books and websites

Day and Night (Nature's Patterns), Anita Ganeri (Heinemann Library, 2004)
The Earth (Space Explorer), Patricia Whitehouse (Heinemann Library, 2004)
The Sun (Space Explorer), Patricia Whitehouse (Heinemann Library, 2004)

www.eas.int
www.nasa.gov/audience/forkids

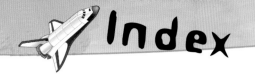

Index